DATE DUE

OCT 27 '95			
DEC 19 '95			

KEEPING MINIBEASTS

WOOD LICE

AND

MILLIPEDES

Franklin Watts, Inc.
387 Park Avenue South
New York, N.Y. 10016

Editor: Hazel Poole
Design: K and Co
Consultant: Michael Chinery

Library of Congress Cataloging-in-Publication Data

Watts, Barrie.
Wood lice and millipedes/text and photographs, Barrie Watts.
p. cm.–(Keeping minibeasts)
Includes index.
Summary: Describes the characteristics and habitats of wood lice and millipedes and discusses how to collect and keep them temporarily for observation.
ISBN 0-531-14162-4
1. Isopoda as pets – Juvenile literature. 2. Millipedes as pets – Juvenile literature. 3.Isopoda –Juvenile literature.
4. Millipedes – Juvenile literature. [1. Wood lice (Crustaceans).
2. Wood lice (Crustaceans) as pets. 3.Millipedes. 4. Millipedes as pets.] I. Title. II. Series.
SF459.I85W38 1991
639'.7–dc20 91–16539
CIP
AC

Printed in Italy by G. Canale & C. S.p.A. - Borgaro T.se - Torino

KEEPING MINIBEASTS

WOOD LICE

AND

MILLIPEDES

Text and Photographs: Barrie Watts

CONTENTS

Franklin Watts

New York • London • Toronto • Sydney

Introduction

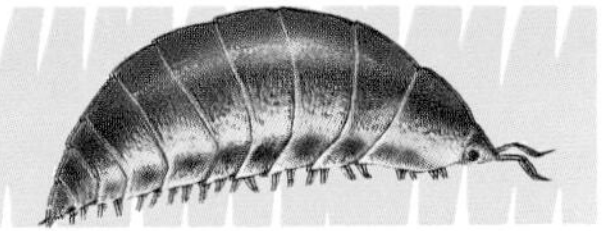

Wood lice and millipedes are small animals that live in the soil and other damp places. They can be found on seashores, in backyards and forests in most countries of the world. They all have a hard shell on the outside of their body which is called an exoskeleton. Wood lice have only seven pairs of legs whereas millipedes can have over 300 legs.

Species

There are many thousands of types of millipede and wood louse. The smallest millipedes are only 2mm long, and the biggest can be over 12 inches long.

Centipedes are often confused with millipedes, but they usually have flatter bodies and longer legs. Centipedes will eat other small animals, which they catch with poison claws surrounding the head, but millipedes eat plants.

Eyes and feet

The easy way to tell the difference between a millipede and a centipede is by the way it moves. Millipedes glide smoothly across the ground, using their many pairs of tiny legs.

Centipedes wriggle and move more quickly as their legs are much larger. Both of them have poor eyesight and find their food by scent. They have a group of simple eyes, called ocelli, on either side of their head.

Habitats

The best time to look for your pets is in late summer or early autumn in damp, woodsy areas. These small creatures are mostly active at night and can be found during the day under logs and branches that are lying on the ground.

You can even create your own habitat by collecting pieces of wood or small logs and leaving them in your backyard. The animals will collect under them.

Collecting your pets

When you find some wood lice or millipedes, why not take them home and study them? Pick them up carefully and put them into a small plastic container with airholes in the lid. Do not collect too many as they could easily damage each other if they are crowded. It is possible to find several different types of wood lice under the same log. See how many you can find. Some are shiny, some are dull, and some have definite patterns.

Creating a habitat

When you get your pets home, you will need a larger container to house them in if you intend to keep them for a long time. Large plastic boxes or plastic pet cages are ideal. Try to create a miniature natural habitat for them in your box.

For this you will need potting soil, dead leaves, and a small log or tree bark. Arrange them just as you would find them in the wild.

Housing

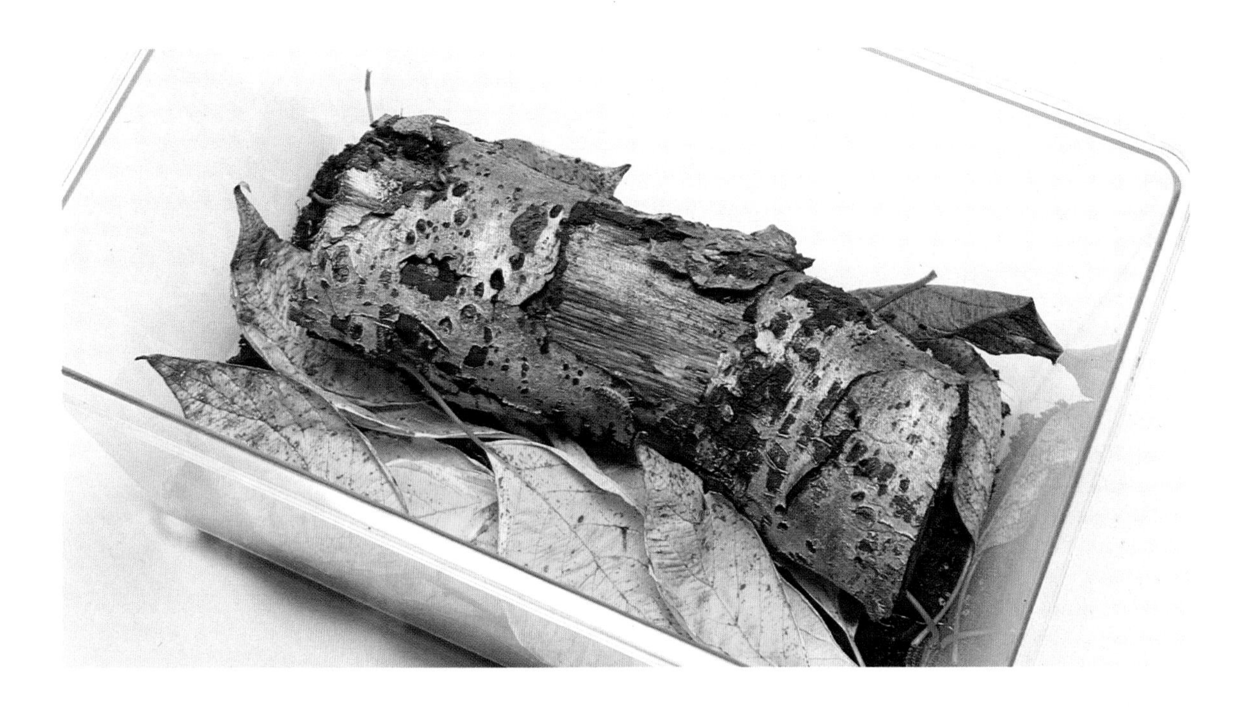

Keep the cage on a windowsill out of direct sunlight. Cover it with a dark cloth. This gives the impression of "night" and will encourage the animals to come out. Carefully remove the cloth and you can watch them. Remember to carefully spray water inside the cage when the soil and leaves begin to dry out, as wood lice and millipedes will die if they are allowed to dry out.

Feeding

After arranging your cage and minibeasts, you must supply them with some food. Most wood lice and millipedes will live happily on a diet of leaves. However, you can also feed them fruit and vegetables. They are very fond of lettuce and thinly sliced carrot.

A hard skin

Wood lice and millipedes have their skeleton on the outside of their body. This exoskeleton is tough and protects them if they are attacked. Pill millipedes, and some wood lice, are able to roll themselves into a ball at the slightest hint of danger. Any predator would find it difficult to get through its armor. Giant millipedes curl themselves up with their head inward when they are threatened.

Baby wood lice

Female wood lice lay their eggs in a pouch on the underside of their body. They are kept moist and are protected with a special liquid until they hatch. A big female wood louse can produce up to 300 eggs at one time. The baby wood lice keep to the underside of their mother's body in the brood pouch until they are well developed. When their skin has hardened, they move away and find food for themselves.

Releasing your pets

When you have finished studying your wood lice, millipedes or centipedes, gently release them where you found them. Do not release any species foreign to that area as they can become pests. Collect some more from a different type of habitat and compare them with your old ones. You will often find certain species prefer to live in a particular place.

Interesting facts

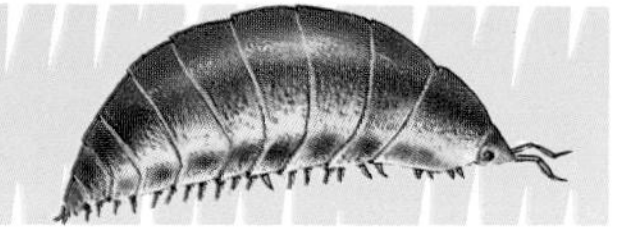

Some kinds of millipedes produce a foul liquid if threatened by predators. One type even gives off a gas that is capable of killing small creatures.

Wood lice need large amounts of calcium to help strengthen their exoskeleton. They are more numerous in chalky soils.

Some male millipedes make sounds at mating time to entice a female to mate.

Certain tropical centipedes have large poisonous fangs. They often bite humans but are rarely fatal.

Most female millipedes and centipedes make little nests for their eggs, and some females guard their nests until the eggs hatch.

Index